LEARN THE VALUE OF

Courage

◆

by Elaine P. Goley

Illustrated by Debbie Crocker

◆

ROURKE ENTERPRISES, INC.

VERO BEACH, FL 32964

Britannica Home Library Service, Inc. offers a
varied selection of bookcases. For details on
ordering, please write:

Britannica Home Library Service, Inc.
310 South Michigan Avenue
Chicago, Illinois 60604
Attn: Customer Service

Library of Congress Cataloging-in-Publication Data

Goley, Elaine P., 1949–
   Learn the value of courage.

   Summary: Presents situations that demonstrate the
meaning and importance of courage.
   1. Courage—Juvenile literature.   [1. Courage.
2. Conduct of life]   I. Title.   II. Title: Courage.
BJ1533.C8G65   1987   179′.6   87-16292
ISBN 0-86592-377-9

Courage

Do you know what **courage** is?

Courage is getting up to roller skate again
after you fall down.

Courage is going to the dentist when you're afraid it might hurt.

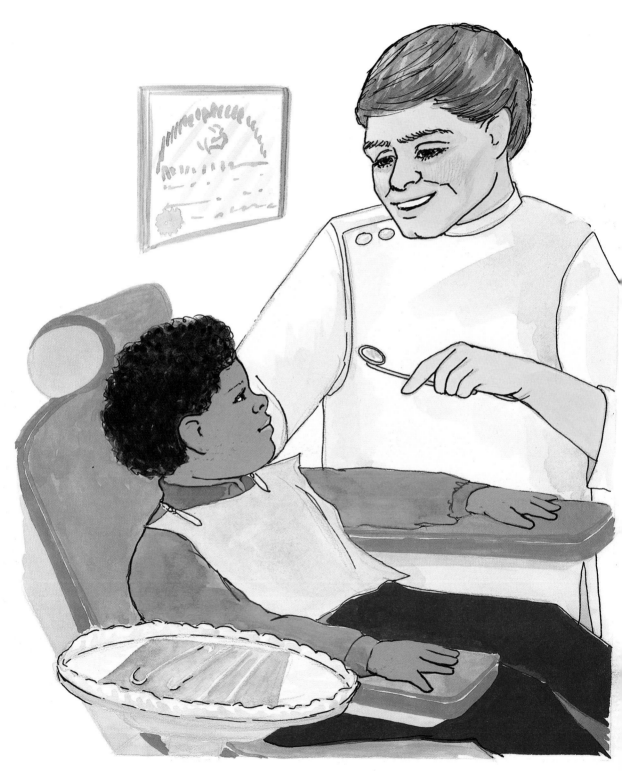

Courage is saying "I'm sorry" when you and
your friend have a fight.

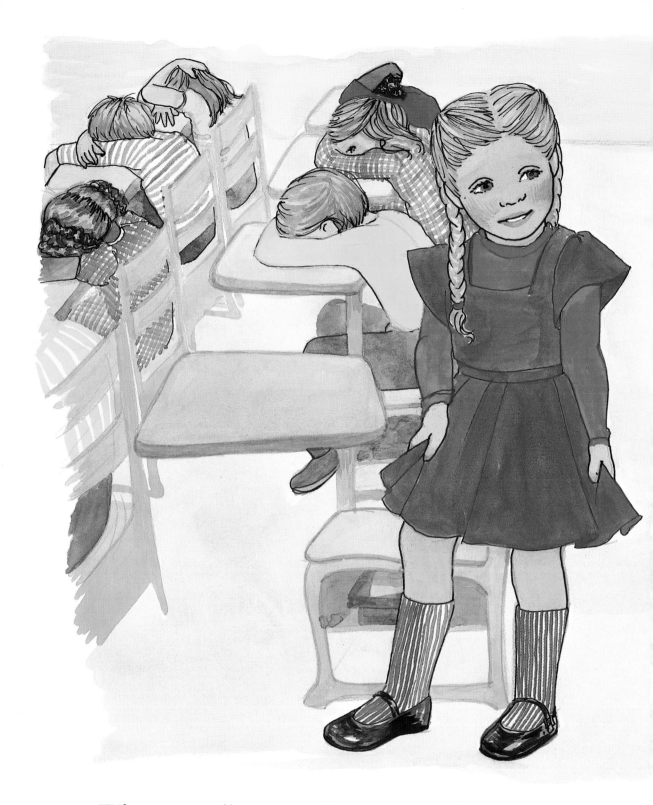

When you tell your teacher you were the one who was talking in class, that's **courage.**

Being nice to your cat even though she scratched you, is **courage.**

Courage is making friends with the new
boy in class.

When you tell your mom that you're the one
who broke the glass, that's **courage.**

Courage is saying "no" when your friend asks you to do something you shouldn't.

Courage is raising your hand to answer a question in class when no one else will.

Refusing to talk to strangers, even if they want to give you a present, is **courage.**

When you let your mom wash your knee after you've skinned it, that's **courage.**

Telling your dad you fibbed about how much
candy you ate is **courage.**

Getting into the water for your swimming lesson,
even if you're afraid, is **courage.**

Courage is trying a vegetable you never tasted before.

Courage is going to your first music lesson
even if you don't know the teacher.

Reading aloud in front of the whole class
is **courage.**

Courage is doing what you know is right.

Courage

Down, down came the rain. CRASH! BOOM! BANG! Thunder shook the house. Lightening flashed through the sky. Jerry sat up in bed.

"Wake up!" he said to his brother, Jimmy.

"What's wrong?" Jimmy asked.

"I'm scared," said Jerry. "I'm going to wake up Mom and Dad. Jerry hopped out of bed. He ran to the door.

"Don't do that," said Jimmy. "Come on, let's sing a song." Then Jimmy began to sing.

"Rain, rain go away. Come again another day."

Jerry opened his mouth to sing. But nothing came out.

"Try again," said Jimmy.

Jerry tried again. It worked! He and Jimmy sang the song over and over. Soon the rain stopped. The thunder and lightening stopped too. Jerry and Jimmy fell asleep.

Which brother showed **courage?**
How can you show **courage** during a storm?

Courage

Mr. Garcia rang his bell. R-r-ring!

"It's playtime," he said. Then all the children put on their coats and went outside. Sara, Tina, and Eve jumped rope.

"Teddy bear, teddy bear, turn around. Teddy bear, teddy bear, touch the ground," sang the girls.

"Hi," said Lois. "Can I play too?"

"No, you're too tall," said Sara. "It's too hard to turn the rope for you."

"And you make too many misses," said Tina.

Eve looked down at her feet. *Lois is my friend too. I'm going to play with her after school today. But what if Sara and Tina find out? Would they ever play with me again?* she wondered.

Finally, Eve put down her end of the rope.

"If Lois can't jump rope, I won't either," she said.

How did Eve show **courage?**
What would you have done if you were Eve?